BOOKWORMS

Animal Homes

A Caterpillar's Tent

Arthur Best

Cavendish Square
New York

Published in 2019 by Cavendish Square Publishing, LLC
243 5th Avenue, Suite 136, New York, NY 10016

Copyright © 2019 by Cavendish Square Publishing, LLC

First Edition

No part of this publication may be reproduced, stored in a retrieval system, or transmitted in any form or by any means—electronic, mechanical, photocopying, recording, or otherwise—without the prior permission of the copyright owner. Request for permission should be addressed to Permissions, Cavendish Square Publishing, 243 5th Avenue,
Suite 136, New York, NY 10016. Tel (877) 980-4450; fax (877) 980-4454.

Website: cavendishsq.com

This publication represents the opinions and views of the author based on his or her personal experience, knowledge, and research. The information in this book serves as a general guide only. The author and publisher have used their best efforts in preparing this book and disclaim liability rising directly or indirectly from the use and application of this book.

All websites were available and accurate when this book was sent to press.

Library of Congress Cataloging-in-Publication Data

Names: Best, B. J., 1976- author.
Title: A caterpillar's tent / Arthur Best.
Description: First edition. | New York : Cavendish Square, 2019. | Series:
Animal homes | Audience: Grades K-2. | Includes index.
Identifiers: LCCN 2017048036 (print) | LCCN 2017054689 (ebook) | ISBN 9781502636508 (library bound)
| ISBN 9781502636522 (pbk.) | ISBN 9781502636539 (6 pack) | ISBN 9781502636515 (ebook)
Subjects: LCSH: Tent caterpillar--Juvenile literature.
Classification: LCC QL561.L3 (ebook) | LCC QL561.L3 B47 2019 (print) | DDC 595.7813/92--dc23
LC record available at https://lccn.loc.gov/2017048036

Editorial Director: David McNamara
Copy Editor: Rebecca Rohan
Associate Art Director: Amy Greenan
Designer: Megan Mette
Production Coordinator: Karol Szymczuk
Photo Research: J8 Media

The photographs in this book are used by permission and through the courtesy of: Photos credits: Cover Chris H. Galbraith/Shutterstock.com; p. 5 Jocelyn Bartone/ Shutterstock.com; p. 7 Ed Reschke/Photolibrary/Getty Images; p. 9 Donna Brunet/Animals Animals/age Fotostock; p. 11 Heather M Clark/Shutterstock.com; p. 13 Johann Schumacher/Oxford Scientific/Getty Images; p. 15 Robert F. Sisson/National Geographic/Getty Images; p. 17 Isabel Eve/Shutterstock.com; p. 19 Jill Morgan/Alamy Stock Photo; p. 21 Andy Reago & Chrissy McClarren/Wikimedia Commons/File: - 7701 – Malacosoma americana – Eastern Tent Caterpillar Moth (14290943841).jpg/CC BY-SA 2.0.

Printed in the United States of America

Contents

A Caterpillar's Home **4**

New Words **22**

Index **23**

About the Author **24**

A caterpillar looks like a worm.

A **tent** caterpillar becomes a **moth**.

Tent caterpillars live in tents.

The tents are in trees.

Many caterpillars live in
one tent.

The tent is their home!

Tent caterpillars begin as eggs.

The eggs are in trees.

The caterpillars **hatch** in spring.

The caterpillars make the tents.

The tents are made of **silk**.

The caterpillars make the silk.

The caterpillars need to be warm.

They sit in their tent.

They sit in the sun.

The tent has many rooms.

Some are warm.

Some are cool.

Tent caterpillars eat many leaves.

They eat the leaves on their tree.

The caterpillars eat more.

They grow.

They can eat all the leaves on the tree!

The caterpillars become moths.

Some lay eggs.

There will be more caterpillars next spring.

There will be a new tent!

21

New Words

hatch (HATCH) Come out of an egg.

moth (MAWTH) A kind of flying bug.

silk (SIHLK) A small thread.

tent (TENT) A soft home made outside.

Index

eggs, 8, 20

hatch, 8

leaves, 16, 18

moth, 4, 20

silk, 10

tent, 4, 6, 8, 10, 12, 14, 16, 20

trees, 6, 8, 16, 18

warm, 12, 14

About the Author

Arthur Best lives in Wisconsin with his wife and son. He has written many other books for children. He sees tent caterpillars every spring.

About BOOKWORMS

Bookworms help independent readers gain reading confidence through high-frequency words, simple sentences, and strong picture/text support. Each book explores a concept that helps children relate what they read to the world they live in.